Entrepreneurial Women

The World Is Your Playground

Disclaimer

Entrepreneurial Women: The World Is Your Playground

This book is published by P&J Publishing Inc. The publishing company can be contacted through their official website, http://pandjpublishing.com/, or email address, pandjpublishing@gmail.com.

The address of publishers is as follows:

2629 E 36th St N
Tulsa, OK 74110

About the Author

Angela K. Chambers is a published Author, Business Coach, Author, and Entrepreneur. She has been successfully managing LasTop Lawn Maintenance and Landscaping Inc., My Jewel Bling, P&J Publishing, LasTop Trucking LLC, 918 Lady Business Blogger, and LasTop Management Company. She is also the proud Co-Founder of Tulsa Black Owned Business Network and Oklahoma Black Owned Business Network.

She aims to support the African American community and motivate females to transform their hobby into an empire through realistic and practical actions.

Angela holds a Master's degree in Entrepreneurial Studies from Langston University. From the same university, she also earned a Bachelor of Arts in Business Administration and received Entrepreneurial training from the Ready Set Go Foundation.

She is really keen on building a network of entrepreneurs. Therefore, she introduced Tulsa BOBN to bring the African American community of Tulsa on a platform where they can network and support each other.

One of Angela's biggest roles, however, is in her company LasTop Lawn Maintenance & Landscaping, Inc. where she used her education and industry experience to gross millions of dollars in revenue for the company. She is also the founder of the LasTop Lawn Care Empire Program.

In this coaching program, she guides entrepreneurs about the strategies and techniques essential in launching and growing a lasting lawn care business. Having seen many companies fail during her career, it is her mission to guide others in finding just as much success as she and her companies have.

Angela serves as Secretary on the Tulsa Black Contractor's Association and Secretary on the Black Women Business Owners of America's boards.

Outside of this and her numerous other roles, Angela enjoys studying the Bible, reading, writing, learning, and traveling. More than anything, and above it all, she loves spending her free time with her husband, children, and grandchildren.

Dedication

Deuteronomy 8:18 (NKJV)

*"And you shall remember the Lord your God, for it is He who gives you power to get wealth, that He may **establish His covenant** which He swore to your fathers, as it is this day."*

In these days, I believe that God has established his covenant with me. Deuteronomy 8:18 is one of my favorite scriptures and was my foundation during the many years of being a single mom. I learned what and who I needed was God. With Jesus as my personal Lord and Savior, I was able to overcome many challenges and situations that could have easily taken me out or left me in a state of despair.

Many years, the first part of the scripture, "...He who gives you power to get wealth" is what motivated me initially. I thought having money would make everything fall into place. Over time, I came to realize while money is good and can help, it can also hurt so the best place to be is in **covenant with God.**

The term **"covenant"** meaning a coming together. It presumes two or more parties who come together to make a contract, agreeing on promises, stipulations, privileges, and responsibilities. In some situations, it means a lifelong agreement.

I am so **thankful** to have LIFE. To be chosen for a time such as this and living on purpose! This book is dedicated to EVERY woman who has fallen and got back up with a mission to be a source for others. I give God all the GLORY!

Acknowledgments

My 106-year-old grandmother, **Wilma C. Phifer Factory Green**, I will LOVE you forever. I realize more and more the strength that you possess and demonstrated all my life. Thank you for loving my unconditionally.

My husband, **Robert Chambers, Sr.,** thank you for your love, continued support with my "many" businesses and other ventures. I am so blessed to continue this life journey with you. I love you.

My girls are the BEST! I love you more and more and am so proud of each of you! **Brittany, Paige, Jennifer, and Jazmin** each of you all inspire me to do better. I love you.

My parents, **Everett & Lois Phifer,** thank you for your love and support.

My number one friends **Darla Viney, LaKesa Mace and Tonya Bowie.** You ladies keep me grounded. I appreciate your forever friendships more than you could ever know.

My grandchildren! I love you dearly. You keep me building my legacy.

I am so very thankful for the connections afforded to me by the founders of the Black Women Business Owners of America, **Aszurdee Sade' and Charity Marcus**. You ladies **ROCK**!

Table of Contents

Introduction

Female entrepreneurship has been on a rise lately. With 42% of all businesses in the US currently owned and managed by females, we can proudly say that women are taking their future in their hands.

Entrepreneurship is no bed of roses. You have to hustle every day to grow your business while strongly dealing with challenges you face along the journey. As a female businessperson, you would need more effort to succeed. After all, the glass ceiling in the corporate world is an established fact.

But despite working day and night to manage their personal and professional life, many female entrepreneurs ignore the factor that can play the most crucial part in success.

Networking!

Do you think it's not important to stay connected with your community and meet new people? Then this book will change your mind by highlighting the importance of community and networking.

It is in human nature to live as a part of society and stay close to other people. If you go against the law of nature, you will end up feeling lonely and anxious. Be it your personal or professional life, you need the support of society to thrive.

While networking is important for entrepreneurs, its value for African American female entrepreneurs can't be stressed enough. Being an experienced entrepreneur, I would advise all aspiring females to never miss any chance to attend community gatherings.

Our community is our strength.

Attending community networking events benefits everyone. Whether you are looking for a new job, need to promote your business, or just want to make new friends, networking events are the ultimate solution. Tulsa Black Owned Business Network, Inc. (TulsaBOBN) is a step in this direction to provide an online networking platform.

The Black community, particularly females tend to face many challenges. But if we continue to support each other, we can claim our due rights in society.

When you run a startup, you want to earn a profit. Let me tell you it is perfectly fine to focus on business growth. But is it a good idea to only think about revenues and forget everything – your family, friends, and community?

The key to becoming a successful entrepreneur as well as a good person is to take time for your loved ones and give back to society in every way you can.

Can't donate huge amounts to charity because you are facing financial issues? Why not network and give your valuable time and advice to people who want to start a business? Who knows you may find a mentor at the same event that will help you resolve your issues and guide you to become an even better entrepreneur!

So, keep this in mind that networking is a two-way road. No one respects a person who only takes and takes. In fact, you may feel ashamed if you continue asking for help and never try to help others. Therefore, your primary goal should be to add value to others. This practice will help you establish lasting connections and will benefit you in the long run.

> *"You can have everything in life you want if you will just help enough other people get what they want."*

Isn't this quote by **Zig Ziglar** an amazing inspiration to start networking and help others?

Another quote by the famous entrepreneur **Russell Simmons** perfectly sheds light on the importance of sharing knowledge:

> *"If you wake up deciding what you want to give versus what you're going to get, you become a more successful person. In other words, if you want to make money, you have to help someone else make money."*

This was a brief overview of the valuable insights I will cover in the next chapters. I want every woman to apply this useful knowledge in their daily life and grow on both personal and professional levels. So, continue reading the book and discover the path to glory!

1. Entrepreneurship and Women

In the modern era, women are making headlines with their profitable startups. A myriad of minority female-owned businesses have come to light in the past 2 decades and managed to make their place in the market and the hearts of consumers through quality products and services.

The founder of FLR-PLN, Adia Dightman, is a Black entrepreneur who aims to change the retail industry by bringing emerging brands on a single platform. Another young and inspiring lady, Vandra Caldwell from Omaha launched Mixins Rolled Ice Cream Parlor with her savings. The business got so successful that now she plans to franchise it.

1.1   Why Women Entrepreneurs Are More Successful

There is no denying that success comes to those who work for it, regardless of their gender. But it's also true that women tend to have certain innate abilities that benefit them during their entrepreneurial journey.

<u>We are good at reading people.</u> This is crucial when it comes to making critical business decisions. I agree that numbers and forecasts are important, but you can't achieve success if you can't read situations. Emotional intelligence can help you establish lasting relationships with clients, vendors, and business stakeholders.

Women become successful because their life doesn't only revolve around their business. Now, I don't want to stereotype, but it is generally observed that women prioritize relationships and their family over their venture. While it isn't easy, women can balance their personal and professional lives better.

Female entrepreneurs face many challenges in their journey and we will discuss some of them a little later. These hardships help us build a thick skin and we can face rejections and setbacks with our head held high.

Females are less egoistic, and their decision-making ability isn't clouded by irrational behavior. We focus on long-term business strategies and opt for tactical approaches to deal with threats that can ruin our entrepreneurial efforts.

Another fact is that women are good communicators and can clearly deliver their thoughts. This trait is greatly helpful when you need to negotiate contracts with suppliers, customers, employees, and other relevant parties.

Also, women's intuition is a real thing. Although we aren't impulsive, we can gauge situations and make the right decisions based on our gut feeling. And I must say it's a blessing upon us!

1.2 Entrepreneurship Is the Right Choice

Entrepreneurship has its fair share of drawbacks. But the pros of launching a startup certainly outweigh the cons.

Starting a business assists in creating a good source of income. You can go on vacation with your loved ones without worrying about receiving phone calls from your boss, asking you to return at the earliest. It gives you the control of your life and offers peace of mind.

When you work as a salaried employee, it is guaranteed that you will receive a fixed salary every month. Entrepreneurship, on the other hand, boosts the earning potential. There is no limit on the potential income, provided that you run your business right.

Being an entrepreneur is stressful at times, but it is also satisfying. When you begin a business you love, you work passionately towards achieving your goals. You get the freedom to work for yourself. Furthermore, you get to learn new things every day which is quite exciting.

Aside from monetary benefits, the non-monetary perks would also entice you to enter the world of entrepreneurship just like Tonya Rapley. She is a proud African American financial expert and the owner of My Fab Finance.

Your business can give you the recognition you deserve. When you introduce products or services to solve problems facing customers, you gain their trust and respect. You get invited to conferences and public speaking events to share knowledge. This amazing experience is priceless.

If you are an entrepreneur or planning to start a business, you may have the idea of how tough it is to stay on top of business activities. However, when you successfully solve problems and meet business goals, you get a sense of achievement that can't be described.

Hence, there is nothing wrong with saying that becoming an entrepreneur is your go-to option due to the plethora of advantages it offers.

1.3   Challenges for Business Women

It is nothing new for females to face challenges in the male dominant society. Despite the weakening patriarchy, female business owners come across many issues they need to handle tactfully.

Running a business is a 24/7 job and maintaining the work-life balance isn't easy. *I second that!* Under such circumstances, you may not find time for your family and friends. But while focusing on your business, it's important not to forget your loved ones.

It has always been a problem for women to find mentors or support. Without the presence of an experienced person, you may find it difficult to solve problems arising in your life. But thanks to the increasing number of female-owned businesses, you can find businesswomen who would guide you in the right direction.

Women are ambitious. No one can deny this fact.

Despite the passion, women sometimes fail to expand the business, manage cash flow, and hire top talent. Do you know why?

It's because they don't always have access to funding sources. Many investors prefer to invest in male-owned businesses. But in recent years, trends are changing.

Moreover, if you lack funds, you can choose a business idea that you can start online or can carry out from home. For instance, you can decide to be a public speaker, sell home-cooked food, or become an online seller.

African American female business owners are not unfamiliar with racial discrimination and gender discrimination. At times, you will experience hurdles that can discourage you. But you can overcome the challenges and prosper if you stay positive and never let negative thoughts and negative people demotivate you.

The solution to most issues that women face during entrepreneurship is networking. For instance, you will find it easier to find a good mentor and gain sufficient business knowledge by attending female-centric networking events. These events can also help you get the required funds for managing business operations.

So, my advice to you is to keep in touch with the community and join as many meaningful networking events as you can. Continue to invest in yourself by attending those events that offer training and information in your areas of weakness.

2. Business Networking

It is a prevalent misconception that business networking is all about attending boring events where people try to promote their brand through tedious sales pitches. Trust me, I wouldn't be this fond of networking if this was the case!

The concept of networking isn't new, though the networking norms have evolved over time. Prior, you could only network in-person, but now the virtual world or the internet makes it more convenient to meet people from around the globe.

The purpose of networking is to meet people and share innovative ideas. It helps to build long-term relationships and offers exposure to knowledge and growth opportunities.

If you network with the community to bombard them with your business cards and other promotional stuff, then it's time you should rediscover networking.

2.1　How Networking Benefits Entrepreneurs

Female entrepreneurs are taking the world by storm. If you want to truly help people around you and have unique ideas, then what are you waiting for? Start your business today. Remember that we are here to unconditionally support you and your venture!

If you already have an established business, then you should never stop striving to further expand it. Aside from looking for financing options and learning about new business avenues, it's important you should never let go of any opportunity to network. I guarantee you it will bring more benefits than you think!

So, before we move forward to the modern-day networking options, let's take a look at some rewards you can reap with this approach:

2.1.1 Builds Reputation

Creating goodwill is essential regardless of whether you run a small business or have hundreds and thousands of employees working with you. As a business owner, you try to steer clear of negative publicity that can ruin your reputation.

Business networking is an unmatched way to build a good reputation. When you connect with your community and businesspeople, always be honest to make a good impression. Once they know you, they will trust your brand.

The competition in the market is tough and you want to stay ahead of your competitors. Your reputation and personal or professional relationships can help you achieve success by buying from you as well as supporting your business.

2.1.2 Increases Visibility

Do you know why businesses spend a huge sum on marketing and advertising campaigns?

It's because they want to stay in the minds of potential customers and build brand awareness. In the competitive market, you can do well if your target audience recognizes your brand and purchases your products and services.

Networking can support this business goal.

When you meet others via networking events, they get to know your brand. You can also guide them on how your products solve their problem. So, when they face problems, they will remember you and become your customer.

2.1.3   Earns Referrals

Despite the availability of so many advertising tools in the era of technology, word-of-mouth is still the most trusted and popular method to promote your business. This is the reason why customer service has become the top priority of the business world.

Put yourself in the shoes of customers and picture this.

When you plan to purchase from a business, you look for online customer reviews. If they have a good rating and internet users say good things about them, you are likely to make a purchase. Then a good experience may drive you to promote that brand in your social circle.

Similarly, you can earn a network of referrals by networking. This will bring in a plethora of potential customers in a cost-effective way.

2.1.4 Boosts Communication Skills

Effective communication is important for small business owners. Females tend to have good communication skills, but you still need to improve business communication if you want to succeed.

During the entrepreneurial journey, you will attend meetings with vendors, customers, and clients. Only through good communication can you negotiate to win.

Networking events give you the opportunity to polish your communication skills. It also boosts confidence and promotes a winning attitude.

2.1.5 Gives More Vendor Options

No matter what business you manage, you need plenty of raw materials or supplies to smoothly run business processes or activities.

For instance, my landscaping empire LasTop Lawn Maintenance and Landscaping Inc. needs lawn care equipment, clothing for employees, paper for office, and other tools. We need vendors to source the needed equipment.

Through networking, you find businesses that can provide supplies for your business. Knowing them personally means you can trust each other and receive fair quotes.

2.1.6 Connect with the Top Talent

Employees are the backbone of a business. They can take your business to new heights with their efforts.

Always remember this golden rule and keep them happy to increase the retention rate.

Entrepreneurs should aim to onboard the talented staff that can add value to business and support business goals. An easy way to get introduced to a talented workforce is to join business gatherings.

It is likely that you will get to know amazing and talented people who would be interested in working with you. So, become a networking master and take the path to growth with the help of the top industry talent.

2.1.7   Find a Mentor

No matter how smart and hardworking you are, you always need expert advice to perform better. The same goes for entrepreneurship where you need guidance to deal with day-to-day challenges. You may not know this but business networking can assist you in finding a sincere mentor.

Female black-owned businesses are doing well and entrepreneurs are ready to support each other. You can connect with experienced professionals and gain invaluable insights into the secrets to success.

2.1.8   Learn About Industry Practices

Many businesses fail every year because they fail to adapt to changing business needs. You can steer clear of such situations by keeping an eye on market best practices.

When you establish lasting connections with industry experts and accomplished entrepreneurs, you find it easier to know what is going on in the business world and rethink your business strategy to avoid pitfalls.

2.1.9   Develop Relationships

The value of friendship can't be explained in words. Your true friends stay with you and support you during tough times. While friendships are important in personal life, your professional life can also benefit from the presence of loyal friends.

Networking provides you with the chance to create a support network. Your network will help you when you feel stressed due to a financial crisis and offer valuable advice to help you better manage the situation.

Entrepreneurship brings along uncertainty. One day you are making profits and the other day, it feels like nothing is working out for you. This is when a mentor and your support network will cheer you up and give the motivation you need to get back on your feet.

Hence, I would advise you to establish a support network of women entrepreneurs, meet them when you can, and support each other unconditionally in your professional as well as personal lives.

Black Women Business Owners of America is now a non-profit organization that I thoroughly enjoying being apart. I look forward to the various trainings and workshops. From finding my CPA to making changes in my operations, this group has definitely been great for my brand.

2.1.10 Give Back to the Community

Black-owned businesses are thriving in the 21st century, all thanks to our Black community. So, as a business owner, it is our responsibility to show them we appreciate their support by giving back to the community.

We should sometimes look beyond making profits and do something for the betterment of society. You can do so by helping others around you whenever you can.

For example, when you get an invitation to a business gathering, then accept the invitation and visit the event with the goal to help at least one person. This may include hiring a person, offering business advice to a novice entrepreneur, or giving a local brand a shout out on social media to help them grow.

Doing something good for others can bring colors to your life. Only by supporting each other can we make this world a better place for everyone.

Find those organizations in your community that are important to you. Organizations with mission statements aligned with your personal life values or affiliation with children, elderly or the environment are usually good fits.

3. Networking in the Modern Era

After overseeing multiple business ventures for years and publishing my first book "**The Journey to Success: Entrepreneurship 101 for Aspiring Women**", the key takeaway I offer to beginner entrepreneurs is that they need to network more.

Knowingly or unknowingly, business people have always utilized networking opportunities to spread the word about their startups. With time, not only have the networking platforms evolved, but entrepreneurs have also got a better understanding of how to add emotional appeal to grow their ventures.

Don't take me wrong. Good entrepreneurs don't try to deceive people by manipulating their emotions. They rather start thinking and feeling like their customers to better solve their problems and make the lives of their audience much easier.

Tanya Memon, a professor at The Ohio State University gives some valuable advice in her TedTalk of 2017. She suggested that networking is a free ticket to a new world. The doors to professional opportunities open when we expand our network and become willing to collaborate with people we didn't know before.

To find promising opportunities for your business, you should attend different networking events. Some of the modern forms of business networking opportunities are as follows:

3.1 Community Events

Despite the amassed use of digital media in every aspect of life, the importance of attending in-person networking events has not decreased. In fact, many female-owned businesses have come together to support each other by regularly arranging such events.

Some professionals may not have good thoughts about these events, since they believe entrepreneurs attend the events for sales purposes only. But if you carefully choose which networking events you must attend, you will find them extremely useful.

Being a minority business owner, it's recommended to focus on Black-owned business events with the intent to meet new people and add value to your loving yet strong community. As the Co-Founder of TulsaBOBN and Oklahoma Black-Owned Business Network (OBOBN), I can tell you that you will receive great support from your community.

Black Women's Expo, Black Enterprise Entrepreneurs Conference, We Buy Black Convention, and similar events regularly take place across the US. You can find information about these events via the internet.

An important thing to know is that you don't necessarily need to go to a conference to network and may find the opportunity at unexpected times.

For example, when you accompany your kids to cheer them in a basketball game, you can talk to other moms about their activities and share details of your business.

Speed networking is also gaining popularity these days where you can meet each attendee for a few minutes and share your business idea and approach. You will find it interesting if you can't attend business events due to the lack of spare time.

3.2   Virtual Networking Events

Networking events are no longer confined in conference halls and community centers. The internet facilitates business owners and job seekers to meet each other no matter where they live.

If you browse the internet, you will get to know that many organizations prefer arranging online sessions where they can meet and greet. It is because the cost of online events is relatively low and you can easily talk to business people from different parts of the world.

Virtual networking events are truly making this world a global village. Aside from meeting other entrepreneurs and vendors, you can also recruit qualified candidates. Instead of wasting time in arranging career fairs, you can invite interested candidates to attend online group meetings and interview them to find the right fit for your company culture.

If you intend to arrange an online networking event for your audience or fellow entrepreneurs, you should keep in mind the following tips to make the event a success:

- Decide why you want to arrange the event
- Set up measurable and realistic goals
- Send out invites to capture the attention
- Spread the word in your community
- Promote the event through in-person meetups as well as digital platforms
- Provide a comfortable environment
- Come up with a contingency plan to deal with unforeseen issues

3.3   Social Networks

When it comes to social media, we often consider it a waste of time. However, networking platforms such as LinkedIn effectively cater to the needs of professionals and business owners.

In this era, joining LinkedIn is vital tool important for small businesses. With over 675 million monthly users, this platform offers the unmatched opportunity to network. It's important to note that your vendors and other partners look for your online presence before signing a contract.

I won't deny the importance of in-person networking, but you can reap more benefits by setting up a personal profile as well as a business page on the website. After that, you should regularly post valuable content to increase brand visibility.

Content posting serves two purposes: the first is to help your followers through insightful posts and the second is to promote your products or services. When you consistently post useful content, your brand stands out and gives you a competitive edge in the market.

You can connect with female entrepreneurs that inspire you and engage with them by commenting on their posts. Just make sure your comments add value to readers.

Apart from free posting, you should also avail the feature of paid ads to leverage the popular platform for your benefit. These advertisement slots aren't costly and enable you to reach your target audience to increase the reach, boost sales, and build followers.

While LinkedIn is the most important platform for business networking, Facebook, Instagram, WhatsApp, TikTok, and other sites can also be of value in this regard.

Videos are the most popular type of content on social media these days. People can consume a lot of useful content within a short time with the help of these videos. You can create videos for video-sharing websites like YouTube. Furthermore, it would also be a good idea to go live on social platforms and interact with your target audience.

Facebook groups also play a major role in business networking. You can join an entrepreneurial group to build friendships. These relationships will be extremely helpful in your journey.

Also, remember to set up a business blog and share your experiences to help the community. This will build credibility and bring traffic to your business page where you can interact with the followers.

3.4   Email Campaigns

No matter what others say, email marketing campaigns have always been effective in marketing. But you should also make them a fundamental part of networking efforts for maximum benefits.

Before, visiting a networking event, you may sometimes know about other attendees. If you have already met any of them, you can send them a quick email prior to the event to show interest in talking to them again.

Similarly, suitable follow-up emails can also do more good than you expect. You may exchange business cards with many entrepreneurs. A follow-up email a few days after the event will make sure they remember you.

You can also ask them to subscribe to your newsletter to get the latest updates about your services. But make sure you don't send them emails until they deliberately subscribe to the list. Otherwise, your well-crafted emails will end up in the spam section.

Another way to network via emails is to send customized emails. You can highlight a real technical issue with their website and offer advice on how to deal with it. This way, you can initiate the conversation and they may acquire your services down the road.

4. Networking Tips

Networking adds great value to business owners if done right. On the other hand, you will end up wasting your time if you fail to grab this golden opportunity. You should stay in touch with your community through networking events as well as digital platforms.

It gives me great pleasure to meet entrepreneurs like you who are always looking for ideas to make their business flourish. To help you out, I have collected some useful tips as well as the common mistakes business owners commit.

4.1 How to Make the Most of Networking

The key to becoming a successful entrepreneur is to believe in yourself and put in your best effort. Remember these key rules when networking and nothing can stop you from reaching your dreams.

4.1.1 Not Every Networking Event Is for You

It's important to carefully choose which networking events you should attend. After all, it is not easy to find time for such activities in your busy routine. For this purpose, you can follow organizations on social media to stay up-to-date with their event calendar.

Personally, I prefer to attend business events focused on female entrepreneurs and I suggest you do the same. It's because this gives you the validation that you are a part of a big community, makes it easier to find suitable funding options, and gives the chance to actively learn and support other females.

4.1.2 Networking Plan

You may attend relevant networking events, stay active on professional social platforms, and regularly talk to other female entrepreneurs in your community. But what good would it do if you don't have a clear plan on how to leverage these opportunities?

You should begin with a strategy and decide what goals you want to achieve. You can also set up some KPIs to measure your performance. For instance, the number of connections you make or total sales generated from these events.

Furthermore, before attending any event, don't forget to do some research about the organization as well as participants you may meet there. Also, carefully choose your attire to make a positive first impression.

4.1.3 Create an Online Presence

Networking is extremely helpful since it helps you build lasting connections and find business owners that are likely to be interested in working with you. But for that, you need to be social and proactively approach them.

You may use Twitter and Instagram for personal use. But did you think about creating professional profiles on networking platforms?

From creating a professional profile on LinkedIn to building a page on Facebook for your business, you should take action to increase visibility.

So, before you begin actively networking with entrepreneurs, it is a must to create an online presence so people can easily find you on the internet and know about your brand.

4.1.4   Prepare an Introduction

No one likes listening to long sales pitches in networking events. If you throw speeches at them, they won't give you a second chance. Instead of being a bother, come up with a brief elevator pitch to introduce yourself.

When you prepare concise statements to introduce you and your business, you can make a good impact and entice them to know you. Moreover, it saves time and allows you to meet more and more people.

4.1.5   Break Free from Your Comfort Zone

Networking events are all about making new connections. You can get in touch with inspiring females working in different industries and share knowledge and ideas. But you are making a huge blunder if you stick only with people you are already friends with.

Meeting new people can make you anxious, particularly if you are an introvert. But it is time you break the chains and get over your shyness. Use this opportunity to meet accomplished entrepreneurs. You will learn a lot by listening to their experiences.

4.1.6 Be Honest

Lying may benefit you in the short-run, but it will never help you grow. When the truth comes out, you will only lose respect in the eyes of others.

Therefore, it's best to be real and truthful at all times. When you network, be truthful about your venture and current business state. If your business is not doing well, some business people at these events may offer you the support you need to rebuild your empire.

4.1.7 Work on Your Listening Skills

The idea behind networking events is to make personal and professional connections. So, don't be selfish and strive to make friends.

Not only should you share your own thoughts and business information, but also be attentive to others. At such events, it is ideal to listen more than you speak. Listen to them and ask intelligent questions to make a good impression and increase knowledge.

4.1.8 Don't Run Away from Follow-Up

And lastly, it's important to follow up with your new connections after a networking event. Don't send them one email after the other, but find a reason to communicate with them again.

For example, you may say that it was nice meeting them and it would be a pleasure to collaborate with them at a given opportunity. Trust me, it mostly works.

4.2 Networking Mistakes to Avoid

Networking is a piece of cake. All you have to do is to attend events and conferences, give your business card to as many people as possible, do everything to impress them, and bam! You are good to go.

Is this how small business owners should network?

Absolutely not! You achieve your business goals when you learn to be a genuine person and don't disturb others with sales pitches. Here are some other wrong practices you should try to avoid:

4.2.1 Ignoring Business Networking

Networking has been a common practice among business communities. Some groups think that it is now outdated and just wastes precious time. Don't think like that if you want to progress.

Without business networking, you will face several challenges that you could otherwise resolve with the help of your social network of female entrepreneurs. Just follow my lead and network the right way to give yourself a chance to succeed.

4.2.2 Spreading Negativity

How do you feel when you meet a pessimist who turns everything into a tragedy? I'm sure their negative energy would negatively affect your thoughts too.

Make it a rule in life to always be positive, no matter how challenging life gets. Keep this rule in mind especially when you attend networking events. You don't want to push people away with your negative mindset. You can share a few problems your business is facing to get advice, but repeatedly talking about those issues isn't a good idea.

Maintain a small smile when meeting professionals and uplift everyone's mood with your positivity. These small gestures make lasting impacts.

4.2.3   Unapproachable Appearance

Not every networking event attendee becomes successful in capturing the attention. Do you know why? It's because of their body language.

You may consider it insignificant, but your appearance, body language, and where you stand during such events is crucial. Before attending an event, choose an appropriate outfit for good first impressions.

Instead of appearing aloof and standing in a corner, go around and meet people you never knew before. Yawning, leaning on a wall or table, and folding arms while listening makes you seem disinterested. Not only should you maintain comfortable eye contact but also use your facial expressions to look interested.

4.2.4   Selling-Oriented Mindset

Don't be like a salesperson that knocks your door at odd times and takes a lot of your time, trying to pursue you to buy their products.

Networking events don't work like that.

Organizations arrange these events to give a chance to entrepreneurs to meet like-minded business people and help each other with challenges they face. Being pushy goes against the goal of these events and causes you to lose the opportunity of making valuable connections.

Your main focus should be on building relationships with entrepreneurs working in diverse niches. You can then convert the leads into customers through a long-term strategy.

4.2.5   Ineffective Follow up Strategy

In every networking event, you may notice some people whose entire focus is on collecting a huge number of business cards. When you give them your info, they spam you with myriads of sales emails.

It is your responsibility to develop a strategy to use the contact information in the right way. Whether you avoid following up with connections after the event or abuse the contact information by repeatedly messaging them, you can't reap the benefits of networking.

What you can do instead is to reconnect shortly after the meeting. I prefer sending a short email or instant message 2-3 days after the conference. This enables me to make friends before I try to sell them a product.

4.2.6   Not Being Helpful

Some entrepreneurs think that the more they ask others for help, the more it will benefit them. This is one of the most common mistakes that you should avoid at any cost.

While networking, you should never focus only on taking and rather try to be helpful. When you add value to others, you gain true happiness.

You should stay active to know your community. If another entrepreneur is having a problem, you can guide them and refer them to another business in your network that can provide them a solution. When you help others, your own problems go away.

4.2.7   Not Asking the Right Questions

Successful business women build contacts with the help of networking events. But if you hesitate in talking to people you are not familiar with and avoid asking useful questions, then these events won't be of any help in your entrepreneurial journey.

What you should do is to be innovative and ask intelligent questions during communications.

An example is that you can ask for their opinion about business laws in your area and share your thoughts too about the topic. This way, you can get to know them and may learn invaluable information.

Just like the main networking event, after-hour events are also important. To fully enjoy the benefits of networking, you should never skip them. Attendees are more relaxed, so you can make friends through informal discussions about mutual interests.

5. CSR Activities

Networking is extremely impactful since it helps entrepreneurs create connections. The rule of thumb for business networking is to do good for the community and in turn, your people will support your venture. This is when CSR comes into play!

CSR refers to corporate social responsibility that obliges businesses to be accountable for their actions. As a result of this model, businesses make sure their activities don't harm the environment or society.

The increasing awareness among the public made it compulsory for businesses to do good for others if they want to stay in business. People, these days, agree to pay a premium price for products if the company focuses on the well-being of people.

For instance, fair-trade businesses charge higher prices than their competitors, but customers agree with the pricing because they know that the additional amount will go to the hardworking laborers that live below the poverty line.

CSR guidelines compel businesses to improve processes and operations to minimize carbon footprint and save the environment. Furthermore, they may invest their profits for the betterment of the people around them.

You don't need to be the CEO of a big corporation to implement CSR. Even small businesses can make an impact with small changes.

5.1 Corporate Social Responsibility: Types

Now that we have discussed the purpose of activities concerning Corporate Social Responsibility, let's explore the different types of this effective business strategy:

5.1.1 Environmental Policies

Many businesses claim their operations are environment-friendly, but they don't always fulfill their promises. You can revise policies about production and waste management to go green.

You should make sure that the waste is properly disposed of so that it doesn't ruin the beauty of nature.

This includes hiring a waste management company to take care of empty boxes, damaged office supplies, and old furniture. Before throwing away the goods, inspect them, and donate the items to charity that are still in usable condition.

If your staff uses personal transport or commutes via the transportation provided by your company, you can promote the use of vehicles that don't pollute the environment. Vehicles should be well-maintained and follow government laws about vehicle emission.

5.1.2 Community Service

The African American community supports each other to deal with challenges such as racism in society. As a business owner, we must give back to them any way we can.

You should arrange career events where your experienced employees guide the enthusiastic young generation about the upcoming professional life. Aside from providing them with valuable advice, you can also offer employment opportunities to talented students.

Along with your staff, you can visit nursing homes and orphanages to share the love with lonely souls and bring smiles to their faces.

It is also important to adopt fair trade practices to depict social responsibility. You can order coffee and tea from fair trade certified vendors that offer organic products.

5.1.3 Labor Benefits

Taking care of employees is also a crucial part of CSR activities. When you take good care of your workforce, they will be able to better focus on their jobs.

Make sure that your employees receive fair compensation for their hard work. Apart from offering them market competitive salaries, you can also share revenue with them in the form of bonuses and rewards.

Keep in touch with the workers and help them out when they face hardships. For instance, if they or their loved ones are ill, you can offer them paid leaves to spend time with their family. This way, they will find it easier to cope up with problems and will remember your generous act.

5.2 Importance of CSR for a Small Business

When people hear the phrase "Corporate Social Responsibility" for the first time, they think this model is only for big businesses. Do you think the same?

If so, then let me tell you this isn't true. CSR activities work for businesses of all sizes and you should adopt these due to the positive impacts.

5.2.1 Community Support

As we have discussed in the earlier sections of the book, community support is critical for small businesses. You can earn their respect and support by helping them in different ways and CSR campaigns can assist you in achieving this goal.

When you improve business processes to save the environment, protect your employees, and do good for the community, you get positive media coverage too, which is essential for business growth.

5.2.2 Customer Satisfaction

Do you know the most common goal for small and midsized businesses? It is to increase the customer base to maximize profits.

If you want to attract customers, you should offer an unforgettable experience. This covers offering quality products and efficient customer service. But this is what other businesses are doing too.

So, how can you stand out?

You can win the market share with the help of your community. When you take action to improve their lifestyle, your community will be more than willing to stick with your brand.

The younger generation is more concerned about sustainable business models. They protest against businesses damaging the environment. You can develop an eco-friendly model to protect the earth for the better future of our youngsters.

When customers are happy with your approach, they also support and promote your brand by sharing their experiences with people they know. This word-of-mouth marketing boosts brand visibility and helps you progress in the long run.

5.2.3   Employee Retention

It isn't easy to find trusted and reliable employees, particularly when you are a female entrepreneur with limited financial resources. So, your focus should be on finding talented staff and retaining them for extended periods.

During the recruitment process, the talented candidates will show a keen interest in working with you if your company observes CSR guidelines. It will help you attract and hire talented staff and build a business profile.

When employees stay with you for long, they understand the organizational culture and support you.

Through CSR, you can increase the retention rate and convince the employees to stay with you.

Employees prefer working with socially responsible businesses because they are aware that the venture always does the right thing. They will stay happy when their needs are fulfilled and their lives have a purpose – to help the needy people and serve the community.

5.2.4   Employee Productivity

The best thing about small businesses is that they are like a close-knit family and treat their employees like family members. *I love this, my dear entrepreneurs!*

When you care for your employees and support them during tough times, they trust you too and stay with you during thick and thin. They eagerly take ownership of tasks assigned to them and become proactive in performing required tasks. An active and supportive workforce can take your business to new heights.

Not only should you offer them monetary benefits, but also provide them an innovative environment where everyone feels free to share their creative ideas. You should listen to them and encourage creativity.

Supporting creativity changes your business for the better. Your employees will come up with ideas that can solve problems your business is facing as well as further improve business processes. So, put your faith in the people working with you and they will be supportive in growing your business.

5.2.5   Cut Down Unnecessary Costs

It isn't easy for female business owners to get funding for their ventures. Your support network will help you find the right funding options, but you should try to keep business costs low for your own good.

Many businesses avoid exploring the CSR field since they believe it wastes money. But you would be surprised to know that investing in CSR can actually save you money if you have a good strategy in place.

A huge amount of your revenue goes waste if you aren't careful. You may end up in losses due to the inefficient use of resources and wastage of supplies.

Implementing policies to protect the environment reduces business expenses. You should abide by laws in your state regarding wastage disposal to avoid hefty fines.

You should also keep track of raw materials and office supplies. This way, you can ensure that there is sufficient stock in the inventory and the equipment doesn't go waste and causes you losses.

6. Sustainable CSR Strategy

Gone are the days when businesses adopted CSR models in an attempt to manage reputation and hide scandals. The world is now relatively transparent and consumers can easily distinguish between real and fake efforts.

Millennials and Generation-Z possess the mindset that businesses should think beyond making profits and do well for people and the environment.

You should learn from the mistakes of corporate giants that lost their wealth since they didn't value common people. It's time you should focus on the well-being of your community and implement CSR strategies to benefit the less-privileged people.

6.1 How Entrepreneurs Develop a CSR Strategy

The major purpose of CSR activities is to preserve nature and support the community. But if you have a well-designed strategy, you will find it easier to effectively pull off these campaigns down the line.

You should begin by analyzing business practices and determining shortcomings. The problem areas may include the use of polluting materials, old machinery that pollutes the indoor air, unjust salary structure for employees, lack of volunteering, gender discrimination at the workplace, and more.

The aforementioned issues negatively affect employee performance and drive your customers away. Thus, you should develop a strategy to vigorously resolve one or more issues. It is also recommended to focus on building the core strengths of the company.

Make sure you set SMART (Specific, Measurable, Attainable, Relevant, and Timely) goals to make the strategy more impactful. With clear goals in place, you can move on to defining steps for implementing the plan and measuring the results through a custom reporting framework that suits your business needs.

The CSR strategy works best when the entire staff is on the same page. For this purpose, communicate in-depth goals and plans with the management and staff and make them understand why this is important.

This approach future proofs your business by earning the trust and respect of your community.

6.2   Impactful CSR Activities

The buying journey of most customers starts with digital media. When they need a product or service, they look for it online. Not only do they want to learn about the features of the product, but they are also interested in learning about the manufacturer.

With a huge number of firms competing in the market for similar products, it's not easy to win customers. But if your target audience trusts you, they will prefer your brand over competitors. The right way to earn their trust is by showing socially responsible behavior.

Startups that actually want to bring a positive change in society pull off CSR campaigns that stay fresh in minds for long. Here are a few of such companies that are doing truly remarkable work:

6.2.1 IKEA

The Swedish company, headquartered in the Netherlands, is mainly known for manufacturing custom furniture and home appliances, but their CSR activities also keep them in news.

IKEA stores currently operate in 52 countries and support local communities through different initiatives. They offer various perks to employees and help them progress in their careers by providing learning opportunities. Inclusion is also a core principle of their strategy and they offer equal employment opportunities.

The company stores mostly work on solar and wind energy and they use recycled materials to produce furniture and equipment. Moreover, the brand regularly donates to organizations working in Africa and other poor parts of the world.

6.2.2 Equinox

Founded in 1991, the US-based fitness company has made its name as a luxury brand assisting clients in living a healthy life. They have been funding cancer research by becoming the founding partner of the Cycle for Survival in 2007.

The Heroes Project is another powerful CSR initiative by the business that supports heroes who fought for our great country. They train the injured veterans for strenuous activities. The Marine Staff Sergeant, Charlie Linville became the first program attendee to climb to the top of Mount Everest.

It would not have been easy for the hero of the United States to achieve this remarkable milestone without the support of Equinox and Tim Wayne Medvetz, the famous adventurer and host of "Everest: Beyond the Limit" TV show.

6.2.3   Ben & Jerry's

The American ice cream producer understands the threats of global warming. Due to erratic temperature change, the water level in oceans is rising, many animal species are getting close to extinction, natural disasters are becoming a common occurrence, and the future of humanity is at risk.

To reduce their carbon footprint, they have evolved their business model to adopt eco-friendly practices. They rely on renewable energy resources for most needs and recycle factory waste with the help of bio-digesters to produce low-cost electricity.

Apart from implementing environment-friendly policies, they also show care for workers via fair trade practices. The company sources raw materials for ice creams from poor communities and pays a fair price directly to workers for their efforts.

6.3   Innovative CSR Campaign Ideas

We can learn from these successful campaigns, but it's never a good idea to copy their tactics. You need to consider your financial status and community behavior to come up with the right strategy for your venture.

You need to make the community your top priority. Only then will you put your best efforts to bring a positive change in society. True change begins at home. You should personally monitor CSR campaigns and invest your time in protecting the environment and people. After that, you can encourage your employees and other business owners to follow your lead.

Take a look at some easy-to-implement ideas that work well for businesses on a budget.

6.3.1   Offer Digital Training

Underprivileged students can benefit from online training. You can teach them some useful skills that would help them improve their financial position. You can also donate smart devices so students can easily access training from remote areas.

6.3.2   Blood Donation Camps

When you save a single life, you save the entire humanity. Arranging blood donation camps can help you do so. You can arrange camps where you and your employees donate blood as well as invite the general public to support you in the sacred cause.

If you are a healthcare service provider, you can also set up free medical camps in the areas where the poor public doesn't have access to healthcare facilities. Your team can guide them about hygiene and health through awareness programs.

6.3.3   Donate Meals

Many people in the world go to sleep on an empty stomach. You can play your role in decreasing hunger from the world by arranging food camps for the homeless as well as those who don't earn enough to provide meals for their loved ones.

6.3.4   Reduce Plastic Waste

Refrain from using disposable coffee cups and water bottles at the workplace. Invest in ceramic cups to reduce waste. Also, arrange filtered water for employees and encourage them to switch to reusable water bottles to play their part in saving mother earth.

6.3.5   Eco-Friendly Lighting

Employees feel lethargic in dimly-lit spaces. So, rearrange your office space to ensure it receives sufficient natural light. Moreover, replace the old lighting system with modern, energy-efficient LED lights that are long-lasting and lower electricity consumption.

6.3.6   Safe Cleaning Products

There are many ways to implement eco-friendly practices such as using natural cleaning products. Not only are they better for the environment, but they also provide a healthy atmosphere for employees.

6.3.7   Install Smart Thermostats

When employees leave their workstations for lunch breaks, HVAC systems still continue to consume energy because no one remembers to turn them off. You can install programmable thermostats that automatically manage the temperature to conserve electricity.

6.3.8   Join Hands with an NGO

Your small business can partner with an NGO known for its philanthropic activities. You can volunteer with them and donate funds to support a good cause and change society for the better.

6.3.9   Arrange a Charity Race

Organizing a charity race is a great CSR activity because it helps you collect donations for a cause and also promotes a healthy lifestyle. Invite the local community to join you and your team and donate profits from the event to an organization of your team's choice.

6.3.10 Support Black-Owned Businesses

We can grow as a community by supporting other local African American businesses. Show your love for your community by purchasing from small Black-owned businesses and motivate your workforce to do the same.

Small businesses owned by African American entrepreneurs are beginning to understand the importance of corporate social responsibility. Regardless of the size and income of your venture, you should strive to add value to the community.

7. Community Involvement Is Good for Your Venture

Community involvement is an extremely valuable asset to small businesses. Consumers conduct brief research about brands before buying their products and around 82% of US people choose brands that do well for society over their competitors.

When you work for your community, you gain their trust and they become your indirect promoters by talking about your positive actions in social gatherings. To make your business a success, you ought to keep your community engaged.

Small businesses attract the audience because they can focus on the needs of individual customers and treat them like family. Unlike business chains, they have a better opportunity to build a community around their business and retain their small but engaged customer base.

Small businesses build impactful relationships with their customers. Their primary focus is on making visitors happy with an unmatched experience. When the focus diverts from earning profits, startups have a better chance of winning life-long loyalty.

Minority-owned businesses tend to struggle in the crowded marketplace, but they can emerge as winners if their community has their back. This means your ultimate motive should be to stay in touch with your community people and support each other at all times.

7.1 How to Engage the Community

We need our community because we can't live in isolation. We need each other's support whether it is our personal or professional life. Keeping this in mind, you should try to be social and come up with suitable ideas to engage people around you.

I agree that it's quite a task to build a community around your brand, but nothing is impossible if you set your mind to achieve a goal.

During my entrepreneurial journey, I have always tried new ideas and learned from my experiences. So, I thought, why not share some of the most effective tips with you that have helped me communicate and make genuine connections with my community?

7.1.1 Stick with Business Values

Entrepreneurs struggle with a myriad of challenges and it may seem an enticing option to exploit customers or try hideous tactics to make the startup profitable. But no matter what others say, you will win in the end when you take the right path.

The first stage of becoming an entrepreneur is to carefully plan and polish the initial idea. At this stage, you define business values and it's important you remember these values during business dealings.

Business values play an important role in developing a company culture. To create a lasting business where employees and customers are satisfied, you can choose from the following core values:

- Honesty and integrity
- Quality products/services
- Prioritizing customers
- Transparency in all actions
- Collaborative environment
- Passion for work
- Accountability for all our actions
- Our suppliers are our partners
- Respect everyone
- Resilience and the will to succeed

7.1.2 Arrange Community Events

Nothing beats the fun and excitement of meeting your amazing community. While attending networking events arranged by other organizations is a good option, you should also arrange such events on your own to establish an even better image of your business.

You can choose a special theme for the meetup so people have something to talk about when they meet each other.

Another way to do this is to mix things up and reserve some time to carry out a donation drive. However, make sure the attendees are notified of this activity via the invitation so they can plan accordingly.

Donate essential items to a reputable non-profit organization working for the betterment of your community and ask your guests to participate in the donation drive. This will definitely help in building a positive image of your firm.

7.1.3   Social Media Activities

The internet has reduced distances and you can talk to your loved ones settled in another corner of the world. The same goes for businesses as they can easily keep in touch with their audience.

If you are yet not active on social media, it is the right time to set up business profiles on social websites that align with your business strategy. Once the pages are ready, you can spread the word to increase awareness about your online presence.

It may take some time to build followership on social media, but you can do so by regularly posting relevant content. Try to create posts that increase engagement. For instance, you can create a poll and ask followers to share their opinions.

You can occasionally share funny images and videos to make customers smile, but be careful to ensure that your content doesn't hurt anyone.

When a user asks a question, provide them the right answer at the earliest. Similarly, when customers post a review, respond to them respectfully regardless of whether it is a positive review or criticism about their negative experience with your business. These steps can help you engage the audience on social platforms.

7.1.4   Be Truthful

It is rightly said that honesty is the best policy. Many people think that business people often lie to hide ugly truths about their ventures. But you can change their perspective by staying truthful and honest.

Be transparent in business dealings and inform customers about benefits as well as potential drawbacks of your products. Similarly, when you are dealing with distributors or suppliers, don't try to cheat them because it will ruin your reputation and give you a guilty conscience. You don't want that, do you?

When you enter the world of entrepreneurship, aim to add value to customers and maintain integrity. If you never forget this golden rule, you will befriend the community and win their trust in no time.

Building a community around your brand and engaging them is a time-consuming task that requires patience. You have to work hard to attract your community and get their support.

Social media and other similar platforms or tools will simplify the task. But, ultimately, it is your kindness towards your community that will capture their attention the most.

Conclusion

African American females tend to be passionate, hardworking, and resilient. These characteristics support them in becoming a better entrepreneur. They deal with challenges that come their way and find their path to success.

Knowing the challenges minority female entrepreneurs face, many women have come together to create support networks. You should strive to do the same and network with female businesswomen in your community to help each other during tough times.

Networking is ideal for aspiring business people since it can help them learn from experiences of others, find the required resources for their ventures, get mentorship, and promote their startup at a fraction of cost as compared to other expensive advertising methods.

Networking not only benefits your business, but also provides a unique opportunity to form ties with your community. You can guide the young talent about entrepreneurship through these events and offer them employment opportunities to build a better future.

To be a better networker, you should attend networking events taking place in your locality as well as join social platforms like LinkedIn to create connections with experienced professionals from around the globe and increase brand visibility.

You need to network with your community to build mutual respect. But at the same time, it's important to invest in CSR activities to show your people that you truly care for them. This will give you the satisfaction of giving back to the community and establish a positive brand image.

CSR campaigns serve many purposes such as reducing waste and carbon emission to protect the environment, taking care of employees, and giving time, support, and donations to deserving people in the community.

You should begin the task by developing a comprehensive strategy as per your business goals to make campaigns fruitful. Small businesses have limited financial resources, but they can still make an impact through continuous efforts.

Becoming an entrepreneur has its own pros and cons. However, you can find success in the long run if you remember your values and stay loyal to the community.

Always do the right thing and make efforts to support your people. It is only possible with the support of the community to grow personally and professionally.

Bibliography

Chen, J. (n.d.). *Corporate Social Responsibility (CSR)*. Retrieved February 22, 2020, from Investopedia: https://www.investopedia.com/terms/c/corp-social-responsibility.asp

Cooper, P. (2020, March 9). *20 LinkedIn Statistics That Matter to Marketers in 2020*. Retrieved from Hootsuite: https://blog.hootsuite.com/linkedin-statistics-business/

CP, S. (2018, June 7). *9 Benefits of Networking in Business*. Retrieved from Medium: https://medium.com/swlh/9-benefits-of-networking-in-business-66b2445e6d84

Cynthia, E. (n.d.). *50 Best Philanthropic (CSR) ideas for Small Businesses*. Retrieved from ProfitableVenture: https://www.profitableventure.com/philanthropic-csr-ideas-small-business/

Goldstein, C. (2020, March 18). *21 Business Networking Strategies for Entrepreneurs*. Retrieved from fundera: https://www.fundera.com/blog/business-networking-strategies

Hayden Field. (2018, April 17). *The Top TED Talks of 2018 So Far -- and What You Can Learn From*

Them. Retrieved from Entrepreneur: https://www.entrepreneur.com/article/312114

Marcus, N. F. (2020, April 21). *Positive Changes for Tulsa's Young Black Professionals*. Retrieved from The Black Wall Street Times: https://theblackwallsttimes.com/2017/04/29/positive-changes-for-tulsas-young-black-professionals/

Prosser, D. (2015, April 20). *Five Reasons Why Women Make Better Entrepreneurs Than Men*. Retrieved from Forbes: https://www.forbes.com/sites/davidprosser/2015/04/20/five-reasons-why-women-make-better-entrepreneurs-than-men/

Russell, K. (2018, June 6). *Why CSR: Four Benefits of Corporate Social Responsibility*. Retrieved from Fronetics: https://www.fronetics.com/csr-four-benefits-corporate-social-responsibility/

Social Impact Statistics You Should Know. (n.d.). Retrieved from Engage For Good: https://engageforgood.com/guides/statistics-every-cause-marketer-should-know/

(2019). *State of Women-Owned Businesses*. United States: American Express.

Made in the USA
Monee, IL
12 March 2022